INTRODUCTION TO ARTIFICIAL INTELLIGENCE

Asif Mehmood

ISBN-13: 9798329155020
ISBN-10: 1477123456

Cover design by: Art Painter
Library of Congress Control Number: 2018675309
Printed in the United States of America

Dedication
This book is dedicated to all those who seek knowledge and innovation in the field of artificial intelligence.

Your Feedback Matters!

Dear Reader,

Thank you for choosing to explore the world of AI with this book. Your opinion is valuable to us! If you enjoyed reading this book or found it helpful, we would greatly appreciate it if you could take a moment to leave a review.

Your feedback helps us to write Second Edition of this book.

Thank you for your support!

[Asif Mehmood]

CONTENTS

INTRODUCTION TO ARTIFICIAL INTELLIGENCE

A rtificial Intelligence (AI) has rapidly evolved from a theoretical concept to a transformative technology that is reshaping industries and societies. This book aims to provide a comprehensive introduction to AI, exploring its history, fundamental principles, applications, and future prospects.

What Is Ai?

AI refers to the simulation of human intelligence processes by machines, especially computer systems. These processes include learning (the acquisition of information and rules for using the information), reasoning (using the rules to reach approximate or definite conclusions), and self-correction. AI can be broadly classified into two types:

1. **Narrow AI:** Also known as Weak AI, this type is designed and trained for a specific task, such as facial recognition or internet searches. It operates within a pre-defined range of functions.

2. **General AI:** Also known as Strong AI or Artificial

General Intelligence (AGI), this type possesses the ability to perform any intellectual task that a human can. AGI remains a theoretical concept, with significant research ongoing to make it a reality.

Importance Of Ai

AI's importance cannot be overstated. It enhances the capabilities of machines, allowing them to perform tasks that typically require human intelligence. This includes decision-making, problem-solving, understanding natural language, and perceiving sensory inputs. Here are some key areas where AI is making significant impacts:

1. **Healthcare:** AI algorithms can analyze medical images, predict patient outcomes, and assist in drug discovery. AI-powered tools help doctors make more accurate diagnoses and personalized treatment plans.
2. **Finance:** AI is used for fraud detection, risk assessment, and personalized financial advice. Algorithms analyze vast amounts of financial data to make predictions and optimize investment strategies.
3. **Transportation:** Autonomous vehicles rely on AI to navigate and make real-time decisions. AI also optimizes logistics and supply chain operations, improving efficiency and reducing costs.
4. **Entertainment:** AI recommends movies, music, and other content based on user preferences. It also plays a role in content creation, from generating music to writing scripts.
5. **Education:** AI personalizes learning experiences, provides intelligent tutoring, and automates administrative tasks. It helps in identifying students' strengths and weaknesses to improve learning outcomes.

Ai Technologies

AI encompasses a range of technologies, each contributing to its overall capabilities:

1. **Machine Learning (ML):** A subset of AI that involves training algorithms to make predictions or decisions without being explicitly programmed. ML uses statistical techniques to enable systems to learn from data.

2. **Deep Learning (DL):** A subset of ML that uses neural networks with many layers (deep networks) to model complex patterns in data. DL has achieved remarkable success in tasks such as image and speech recognition.

3. **Natural Language Processing (NLP):** A field of AI that focuses on the interaction between computers and humans through natural language. NLP enables machines to understand, interpret, and generate human language.

4. **Computer Vision:** An area of AI that enables machines to interpret and understand visual information from the world. This includes tasks such as image recognition, object detection, and facial recognition.

5. **Reinforcement Learning (RL):** A type of ML where an agent learns to make decisions by taking actions in an environment to maximize cumulative reward. RL is widely used in robotics and game playing.

Challenges And Ethical Considerations

While AI offers numerous benefits, it also poses several challenges and ethical concerns:

1. **Bias and Fairness:** AI systems can inherit biases present in the training data, leading to unfair or discriminatory

outcomes. Ensuring fairness and equity in AI systems is a critical issue.

2. **Privacy:** AI often requires large amounts of data, raising concerns about data privacy and security. Protecting individuals' privacy while leveraging data for AI applications is a significant challenge.

3. **Job Displacement:** Automation powered by AI can lead to job displacement in various sectors. Balancing technological advancement with employment and economic stability is essential.

4. **Transparency and Accountability:** AI systems can be complex and opaque, making it difficult to understand their decision-making processes. Ensuring transparency and accountability in AI systems is crucial for trust and reliability.

5. **Regulation:** Developing appropriate regulatory frameworks for AI that encourage innovation while safeguarding public interest is a complex task.

Conclusion

Artificial Intelligence is a powerful and rapidly evolving field with the potential to transform numerous aspects of our lives. This book aims to provide a detailed exploration of AI, from its foundational principles to its diverse applications and future prospects. As we delve deeper into the world of AI, we will uncover the remarkable possibilities it offers and the challenges we must navigate to harness its full potential.

CHAPTER 1: INTRODUCTION TO ARTIFICIAL INTELLIGENCE

Artificial Intelligence (AI) is a branch of computer science that aims to create machines capable of intelligent behavior. The field has a rich history and encompasses a variety of subfields, including machine learning, neural networks, natural language processing, and robotics. This chapter provides an in-depth introduction to AI, its definitions, key concepts, and the underlying technologies that drive its development.

Definition and Scope of AI

Artificial Intelligence can be defined in multiple ways, but it generally refers to the ability of a machine to perform tasks that typically require human intelligence. These tasks include reasoning, learning, problem-solving, perception, and language understanding. AI can be categorized into two types:

1. **Narrow AI (Weak AI):** This type of AI is designed to perform a specific task, such as voice recognition or chess playing. It operates under a narrow set of constraints and is not capable of generalizing its knowledge to other domains.

2. **General AI (Strong AI or AGI):** This type of AI has the ability to understand, learn, and apply knowledge in a

generalized way across a wide range of tasks, similar to human cognitive abilities. While narrow AI is currently in widespread use, general AI remains a theoretical goal for researchers.

Historical Background

The concept of artificial intelligence dates back to ancient times, but the formal foundation was laid in the mid-20th century. Key milestones in the history of AI include:

1. **1943:** Warren McCulloch and Walter Pitts developed the first conceptual model of a neural network, which laid the groundwork for later developments in machine learning and neural networks.
2. **1950:** Alan Turing proposed the Turing Test as a measure of machine intelligence in his seminal paper "Computing Machinery and Intelligence."
3. **1956:** The term "Artificial Intelligence" was coined by John McCarthy during the Dartmouth Conference, which is considered the birth of AI as an academic discipline.
4. **1960s-1970s:** Early AI research focused on symbolic reasoning and problem-solving, leading to the development of programs like ELIZA (a natural language processing program) and SHRDLU (a program capable of understanding natural language in a limited domain).
5. **1980s-1990s:** The rise of expert systems, which used rules and knowledge bases to simulate the decision-making abilities of human experts, marked a significant advancement in AI applications.
6. **2000s-Present:** The advent of big data, increased computational power, and advances in machine learning and neural networks have driven a resurgence in AI research and applications, leading

to breakthroughs in areas such as image and speech recognition, autonomous vehicles, and natural language processing.

Key Concepts in AI

1. **Machine Learning (ML):** A subset of AI that involves training algorithms to learn from and make predictions based on data. ML can be further divided into supervised learning (learning from labeled data), unsupervised learning (learning from unlabeled data), and reinforcement learning (learning through trial and error).

2. **Neural Networks:** Inspired by the structure and function of the human brain, neural networks are a key technology in AI. They consist of interconnected nodes (neurons) that process information in layers, enabling the recognition of complex patterns in data.

3. **Natural Language Processing (NLP):** A field of AI that focuses on the interaction between computers and humans through natural language. NLP enables machines to understand, interpret, and generate human language.

4. **Computer Vision:** The ability of machines to interpret and understand visual information from the world, including images and videos. Computer vision is used in applications such as facial recognition, object detection, and autonomous driving.

5. **Reinforcement Learning (RL):** A type of machine learning where an agent learns to make decisions by taking actions in an environment to maximize cumulative reward. RL is widely used in robotics, game playing, and autonomous systems.

Applications of AI

AI has a wide range of applications across various industries, including:

1. **Healthcare:** AI is used for medical diagnosis, personalized treatment plans, drug discovery, and predictive analytics to improve patient outcomes and reduce costs.

2. **Finance:** AI algorithms are employed for fraud detection, algorithmic trading, risk management, and personalized financial advice.

3. **Transportation:** AI powers autonomous vehicles, optimizes traffic management systems, and enhances logistics and supply chain operations.

4. **Entertainment:** AI personalizes content recommendations, automates content creation, and powers virtual assistants and chatbots.

5. **Education:** AI enables personalized learning experiences, intelligent tutoring systems, and automated grading and administrative tasks.

Ethical and Societal Implications

As AI continues to advance, it raises important ethical and societal questions that must be addressed. These include:

1. **Bias and Fairness:** Ensuring that AI systems do not perpetuate or exacerbate existing biases in society.

2. **Privacy:** Protecting individuals' data privacy while enabling the use of large datasets for AI training.

3. **Job Displacement:** Addressing the potential impact of AI-driven automation on employment and workforce dynamics.

4. **Transparency and Accountability:** Ensuring that AI systems are transparent, explainable, and accountable for their decisions and actions.

Future Directions

The future of AI holds immense potential, with ongoing research and development aimed at achieving more advanced and generalized AI capabilities. Key areas of focus include:

1. **General AI:** Advancing towards the development of AI systems that possess human-like cognitive abilities and can perform a wide range of tasks.

2. **Human-AI Collaboration:** Enhancing the ability of AI systems to work collaboratively with humans, augmenting human capabilities and improving decision-making processes.

3. **Ethical AI:** Developing frameworks and guidelines to ensure the ethical and responsible use of AI technologies.

4. **AI in Society:** Exploring the broader societal impacts of AI and how it can be harnessed to address global challenges such as climate change, healthcare, and education.

In conclusion, AI represents a transformative technology with the potential to revolutionize various aspects of our lives. This book will delve deeper into the various facets of AI, exploring its history, fundamental principles, applications, and future prospects. As we embark on this journey, we will uncover the remarkable possibilities that AI offers and the challenges we must navigate to harness its full potential.

CHAPTER 2:
HISTORY OF AI

The history of Artificial Intelligence (AI) is a fascinating journey that spans centuries, from early philosophical inquiries to the cutting-edge technologies of today. This chapter delves into the key milestones, breakthroughs, and influential figures that have shaped the development of AI.

Early Concepts and Philosophical Foundations

The idea of creating artificial beings with human-like intelligence can be traced back to ancient mythology and philosophical writings:

1. **Ancient Mythology:** Stories of intelligent automata and mechanical beings appear in various cultures. For example, ancient Greek mythology includes tales of Talos, a giant automaton built to protect Crete, and Pygmalion, who created a statue that came to life.

2. **Philosophical Foundations:** Early philosophers such as Aristotle pondered the nature of intelligence and the possibility of creating artificial beings. In the 17th century, René Descartes and Thomas Hobbes speculated about mechanical reasoning and the potential for artificial intelligence.

The Birth of AI as a Discipline

The formal establishment of AI as an academic discipline

occurred in the mid-20th century, marked by several key events and figures:

1. **1943:** Warren McCulloch and Walter Pitts published a seminal paper on neural networks, proposing a mathematical model for artificial neurons. This work laid the groundwork for later developments in neural networks and machine learning.

2. **1950:** Alan Turing, a British mathematician and logician, published his landmark paper "Computing Machinery and Intelligence." Turing introduced the concept of the Turing Test, a criterion for determining whether a machine can exhibit intelligent behavior indistinguishable from that of a human.

3. **1956:** The Dartmouth Conference, organized by John McCarthy, Marvin Minsky, Nathaniel Rochester, and Claude Shannon, is considered the birth of AI as a field of study. The conference brought together leading researchers to discuss the potential of machine intelligence and laid the foundation for future AI research.

Early AI Research and Developments

The early years of AI research focused on symbolic reasoning, problem-solving, and game playing. Key developments during this period include:

1. **1950s-1960s:** Researchers developed early AI programs such as the Logic Theorist (1955) by Allen Newell and Herbert A. Simon, which could prove mathematical theorems, and ELIZA (1966) by Joseph Weizenbaum, a natural language processing program that simulated conversation.

2. **1960s-1970s:** The development of expert systems, which used rule-based knowledge to simulate the decision-making abilities of human experts, marked a significant advancement. Notable examples include

DENDRAL (1965), a program for chemical analysis, and MYCIN (1972), a medical diagnosis system.

3. **1970s-1980s:** The rise of knowledge-based systems and the development of languages such as LISP and Prolog facilitated AI research. However, this period also saw the "AI winter," characterized by reduced funding and interest due to unmet expectations and technical limitations.

The Renaissance of AI

The resurgence of AI in the 21st century can be attributed to several factors, including advances in computational power, the availability of large datasets, and breakthroughs in machine learning:

1. **1990s:** AI research gained momentum with significant achievements such as IBM's Deep Blue defeating world chess champion Garry Kasparov in 1997, showcasing the potential of AI in complex problem-solving.

2. **2000s:** The advent of big data and the proliferation of the internet provided vast amounts of data for training AI models. Advances in machine learning, particularly deep learning, led to remarkable progress in tasks such as image and speech recognition.

3. **2010s:** The development of deep learning algorithms, inspired by the structure and function of the human brain, revolutionized AI. Notable achievements include the creation of convolutional neural networks (CNNs) for image processing and recurrent neural networks (RNNs) for sequential data analysis.

4. **2016:** Google's AlphaGo, developed by DeepMind, defeated world champion Go player Lee Sedol, demonstrating the power of reinforcement learning and deep neural networks in mastering complex games.

Current State and Future Directions

Today, AI is an integral part of many industries and continues to evolve at a rapid pace. Key areas of focus include:

1. **Machine Learning and Deep Learning:** Ongoing research aims to improve the efficiency, interpretability, and generalization capabilities of machine learning models.

2. **Natural Language Processing:** Advances in NLP enable machines to understand and generate human language with increasing accuracy, powering applications such as chatbots, virtual assistants, and language translation.

3. **Autonomous Systems:** AI is driving the development of autonomous vehicles, drones, and robotics, with significant implications for transportation, logistics, and manufacturing.

4. **Ethics and Governance:** As AI becomes more pervasive, addressing ethical concerns and establishing regulatory frameworks are critical to ensuring its responsible and beneficial use.

Conclusion

The history of AI is a testament to human ingenuity and the relentless pursuit of knowledge. From early philosophical musings to the groundbreaking achievements of today, AI has come a long way. As we continue to explore the frontiers of AI, it is essential to draw lessons from the past and remain mindful of the ethical and societal implications. The journey of AI is far from over, and the future holds exciting possibilities for further advancements and transformative applications.

CHAPTER 3: FUNDAMENTALS OF MACHINE LEARNING

Machine learning (ML) is a subset of artificial intelligence (AI) that focuses on the development of algorithms and statistical models that enable computers to perform specific tasks without using explicit instructions. It relies on patterns and inference instead. This chapter will delve into the fundamental concepts, types, and applications of machine learning.

What is Machine Learning?

Machine learning involves training a model on a dataset to make predictions or decisions without being explicitly programmed to perform the task. This process involves:

1. **Data Collection:** Gathering data relevant to the problem.
2. **Data Preprocessing:** Cleaning and organizing the data for use.
3. **Model Training:** Using the data to train a machine learning model.
4. **Model Evaluation:** Testing the model to assess its accuracy.
5. **Prediction/Inference:** Using the model to make predictions on new data.

Types of Machine Learning

Machine learning can be broadly classified into three categories: supervised learning, unsupervised learning, and reinforcement learning.

Supervised Learning

Supervised learning involves training a model on a labeled dataset, meaning the input data is paired with the correct output. The goal is to learn a mapping from inputs to outputs. Common tasks include:

- **Classification:** Assigning inputs to predefined categories. For example, classifying emails as spam or non-spam.
- **Regression:** Predicting a continuous value. For example, predicting house prices based on various features.

Example: Suppose we want to predict whether an email is spam. The input features could include the presence of certain keywords, the length of the email, and the sender's address. The output is a label indicating whether the email is spam or not. The model is trained on a dataset of labeled emails to learn the patterns associated with spam emails.

Unsupervised Learning

Unsupervised learning deals with unlabeled data. The goal is to infer the natural structure present within a set of data points. Common tasks include:

- **Clustering:** Grouping data points into clusters based on similarity. For example, customer segmentation in marketing.
- **Dimensionality Reduction:** Reducing the number of features in a dataset while preserving important information. For example, principal component analysis (PCA).

Example: In clustering, we might have a dataset of customer purchase histories. The algorithm groups customers into clusters based on their purchase behavior, helping businesses to identify distinct customer segments and tailor marketing strategies accordingly.

Reinforcement Learning

Reinforcement learning involves training an agent to make a sequence of decisions by rewarding desired behaviors and/or punishing undesired ones. The agent learns to maximize cumulative rewards in a given environment.

Example: In a game-playing scenario, the agent receives positive rewards for winning points and negative rewards for losing points. Over time, the agent learns to develop strategies that maximize its score.

Key Algorithms in Machine Learning

Several algorithms are commonly used in machine learning, each with its strengths and weaknesses. Here are a few notable ones:

Linear Regression

Linear regression is used for regression tasks. It models the relationship between a dependent variable and one or more independent variables by fitting a linear equation to observed data.

Example: Predicting house prices based on features such as square footage, number of bedrooms, and location.

Decision Trees

Decision trees are used for both classification and regression tasks. They split the data into branches based on feature values, leading to a decision at each leaf node.

Example: Classifying whether a loan applicant is high or low risk based on features like credit score, income, and employment history.

Support Vector Machines (SVM)

SVMs are used for classification tasks. They find the hyperplane that best separates data points of different classes.

Example: Classifying emails as spam or not spam.

Neural Networks

Neural networks are a set of algorithms modeled after the human brain. They are used for a variety of tasks, including image and speech recognition.

Example: Identifying objects in images.

K-Means Clustering

K-means is an unsupervised learning algorithm used for clustering tasks. It partitions the dataset into K clusters, where each data point belongs to the cluster with the nearest mean.

Example: Segmenting customers into distinct groups based on purchasing behavior.

Applications of Machine Learning

Machine learning has a wide range of applications across various industries:

1. **Healthcare:** Predictive analytics for patient outcomes, disease diagnosis, personalized treatment plans, and drug discovery.
2. **Finance:** Fraud detection, risk management, algorithmic trading, and personalized financial services.
3. **Retail:** Customer segmentation, inventory management, and recommendation systems.
4. **Manufacturing:** Predictive maintenance, quality control, and supply chain optimization.
5. **Transportation:** Autonomous vehicles, traffic prediction, and route optimization.

Challenges in Machine Learning

Despite its potential, machine learning faces several challenges:

1. **Data Quality:** The accuracy of machine learning models heavily depends on the quality of the data. Noisy or incomplete data can lead to poor model performance.
2. **Overfitting:** When a model learns the training data too well, it may perform poorly on new, unseen data. Regularization techniques and cross-validation are used to mitigate overfitting.
3. **Interpretability:** Complex models, such as deep neural networks, can be difficult to interpret and understand. Techniques for explainable AI aim to make these models more transparent.
4. **Scalability:** Handling large datasets and complex models requires significant computational resources. Efficient algorithms and distributed computing frameworks are essential for scalability.

Future Directions in Machine Learning

The future of machine learning holds exciting possibilities:

1. **Automated Machine Learning (AutoML):** Tools and frameworks that automate the process of model selection, hyperparameter tuning, and feature engineering, making machine learning more accessible.
2. **Federated Learning:** A collaborative approach to training models across decentralized devices while preserving data privacy.
3. **Interdisciplinary Applications:** Combining machine learning with other fields, such as biology, physics, and social sciences, to solve complex problems.
4. **Ethical AI:** Developing guidelines and frameworks to

ensure the ethical use of machine learning, addressing issues such as bias, fairness, and accountability.

Conclusion

Machine learning is a powerful and versatile tool that is transforming industries and driving innovation. Understanding the fundamental concepts, types, algorithms, and applications of machine learning is essential for harnessing its potential. As we continue to advance in this field, addressing the challenges and ethical considerations will be crucial to ensuring that machine learning benefits society as a whole.

CHAPTER 4: DEEP LEARNING AND NEURAL NETWORKS

Deep learning is a subset of machine learning that focuses on neural networks with many layers (deep networks) to model complex patterns in data. This chapter explores the principles of deep learning, the structure and function of neural networks, and their applications.

What is Deep Learning?

Deep learning involves training large neural networks on vast amounts of data to learn complex representations and patterns. Unlike traditional machine learning algorithms, which rely on hand-crafted features, deep learning automatically learns features from the data.

Structure of Neural Networks

Neural networks consist of interconnected nodes (neurons) organized in layers:

1. **Input Layer:** The input layer receives the raw data.
2. **Hidden Layers:** Hidden layers perform computations and transformations on the data. Deep networks have multiple hidden layers, allowing them to learn hierarchical representations.
3. **Output Layer:** The output layer produces the final prediction or classification.

Each connection between neurons has a weight that is adjusted during training to minimize the error between the predicted and actual outputs.

Activation Functions

Activation functions introduce non-linearity into the network, enabling it to learn complex patterns. Common activation functions include:

1. **Sigmoid:** Outputs values between 0 and 1. Useful for binary classification tasks.
2. **Tanh:** Outputs values between -1 and 1. Used in hidden layers.
3. **ReLU (Rectified Linear Unit):** Outputs the input directly if positive, otherwise zero. Commonly used in hidden layers due to its computational efficiency.

Training Neural Networks

Training a neural network involves the following steps:

1. **Forward Propagation:** Passing the input data through the network to obtain the output.
2. **Loss Function:** Calculating the error between the predicted and actual outputs using a loss function (e.g., mean squared error, cross-entropy).
3. **Backpropagation:** Computing the gradients of the loss function with respect to the weights and updating the weights using optimization algorithms (e.g., stochastic gradient descent).

Types of Neural Networks

There are several types of neural networks, each suited for different tasks:

1. **Feedforward Neural Networks:** The simplest type of neural network, where information moves in one

direction from input to output.

2. **Convolutional Neural Networks (CNNs):** Specialized for processing grid-like data such as images. They use convolutional layers to extract spatial features.

3. **Recurrent Neural Networks (RNNs):** Designed for sequential data such as time series or natural language. They have loops that allow information to persist.

4. **Generative Adversarial Networks (GANs):** Consist of two networks (a generator and a discriminator) that compete against each other. GANs are used for generating realistic data samples.

Applications of Deep Learning

Deep learning has revolutionized many fields with its ability to learn from large datasets:

1. **Image Recognition:** CNNs are used for tasks such as object detection, image classification, and facial recognition.

2. **Natural Language Processing:** RNNs and transformers are used for tasks such as language translation, sentiment analysis, and text generation.

3. **Speech Recognition:** Deep learning models convert spoken language into text and improve voice-controlled applications.

4. **Autonomous Vehicles:** Deep learning is used for perception, decision-making, and control in self-driving cars.

5. **Healthcare:** Deep learning assists in medical image analysis, disease prediction, and personalized treatment plans.

Challenges in Deep Learning

Despite its successes, deep learning faces several challenges:

1. **Data Requirements:** Deep learning models require large amounts of labeled data, which can be expensive and time-consuming to obtain.

2. **Computational Resources:** Training deep networks is computationally intensive and requires powerful hardware such as GPUs.

3. **Interpretability:** Deep learning models are often seen as "black boxes" due to their complexity, making it difficult to understand how they make decisions.

4. **Overfitting:** Deep networks are prone to overfitting, especially when trained on small datasets. Regularization techniques and dropout are used to mitigate overfitting.

Future Directions in Deep Learning

The future of deep learning holds exciting possibilities:

1. **Few-Shot Learning:** Developing models that can learn from a small number of examples.

2. **Explainable AI:** Creating models that provide interpretable and understandable explanations for their decisions.

3. **Transfer Learning:** Leveraging pre-trained models on related tasks to reduce the need for large labeled datasets.

4. **Neuro-Symbolic AI:** Combining neural networks with symbolic reasoning to enhance learning and decision-making.

Conclusion

Deep learning has made significant strides in various fields, offering powerful tools for learning complex patterns and making accurate predictions. Understanding the structure, function, and applications of neural networks is essential for harnessing the potential of deep learning. As the field continues to evolve, addressing the challenges and exploring new directions will be crucial for further advancements and impactful applications.

CHAPTER 5: NATURAL LANGUAGE PROCESSING

Natural Language Processing (NLP) is a subfield of AI that focuses on the interaction between computers and human language. This chapter explores the fundamental concepts, techniques, and applications of NLP.

What is Natural Language Processing?

NLP involves enabling computers to understand, interpret, and generate human language. It encompasses a wide range of tasks, including:

1. **Text Analysis:** Extracting meaningful information from text data.
2. **Language Generation:** Creating coherent and contextually relevant text.
3. **Translation:** Converting text from one language to another.
4. **Speech Recognition:** Converting spoken language into text.

Key Techniques in NLP

Several techniques are commonly used in NLP, including:

1. **Tokenization:** Breaking down text into individual

words or tokens.

2. **Part-of-Speech Tagging:** Identifying the grammatical parts of speech in a sentence.

3. **Named Entity Recognition (NER):** Identifying and classifying entities such as names, dates, and locations in text.

4. **Sentiment Analysis:** Determining the sentiment or emotional tone of text.

5. **Machine Translation:** Translating text from one language to another using models such as Google Translate.

NLP Algorithms and Models

NLP relies on various algorithms and models to perform its tasks:

1. **Rule-Based Systems:** Early NLP systems used handcrafted rules and heuristics to process language. While simple, they lacked flexibility and scalability.

2. **Statistical Models:** Statistical methods, such as n-grams and Hidden Markov Models (HMMs), leverage probabilistic approaches to model language.

3. **Machine Learning Models:** Supervised learning algorithms, such as Naive Bayes and Support Vector Machines (SVMs), are used for tasks like text classification and sentiment analysis.

4. **Deep Learning Models:** Advanced models, such as recurrent neural networks (RNNs), long short-term memory networks (LSTMs), and transformers, have revolutionized NLP by achieving state-of-the-art performance on various tasks.

Applications of NLP

NLP has numerous applications across different industries:

1. **Customer Service:** Chatbots and virtual assistants use

NLP to understand and respond to customer queries.

2. **Healthcare:** NLP is used for extracting information from medical records, aiding in diagnosis, and personalizing treatment plans.

3. **Finance:** Analyzing financial news, automating customer support, and detecting fraudulent activities.

4. **Marketing:** Sentiment analysis to gauge customer opinions, content generation, and personalized recommendations.

5. **Education:** Automated grading, plagiarism detection, and personalized learning experiences.

Challenges in NLP

NLP faces several challenges that researchers and practitioners must address:

1. **Ambiguity:** Human language is inherently ambiguous, with words and sentences often having multiple meanings.

2. **Context Understanding:** Understanding the context in which words and sentences are used is crucial for accurate interpretation.

3. **Multilingual Processing:** Developing models that can handle multiple languages and dialects effectively.

4. **Bias and Fairness:** Ensuring that NLP systems do not perpetuate or amplify biases present in the training data.

Future Directions in NLP

The future of NLP holds promising developments:

1. **Universal Language Models:** Developing models that can understand and generate multiple languages with high accuracy.

2. **Contextual Understanding:** Enhancing models' ability

to understand and generate contextually relevant and coherent text.

3. **Ethical NLP:** Creating frameworks to ensure the ethical use of NLP technologies, addressing issues such as privacy, bias, and fairness.

4. **Human-AI Collaboration:** Improving the ability of NLP systems to work collaboratively with humans, augmenting human capabilities and enhancing decision-making processes.

Conclusion

Natural Language Processing is a critical area of AI that enables machines to understand and interact with human language. By exploring the fundamental concepts, techniques, and applications of NLP, we gain insights into how this technology is transforming various industries and improving our daily lives. As the field continues to advance, addressing the challenges and exploring new directions will be essential for further progress and impactful applications.

CHAPTER 6: REINFORCEMENT LEARNING

Reinforcement Learning (RL) is a branch of machine learning that focuses on training agents to make decisions by interacting with an environment. This chapter delves into the principles of reinforcement learning, its key components, and its applications.

What is Reinforcement Learning?

Reinforcement learning involves training an agent to take actions in an environment to maximize cumulative rewards. Unlike supervised learning, where the model learns from labeled data, RL relies on trial and error to discover the best actions.

Key Components of Reinforcement Learning

RL involves several key components:

1. **Agent:** The decision-maker that interacts with the environment.
2. **Environment:** The external system with which the agent interacts.
3. **State:** A representation of the current situation or configuration of the environment.
4. **Action:** The set of possible moves or decisions the agent can make.

5. **Reward:** A feedback signal received by the agent after taking an action, indicating the success or failure of that action.

6. **Policy:** A strategy or mapping from states to actions that the agent follows.

7. **Value Function:** A function that estimates the expected cumulative reward of being in a particular state or taking a specific action.

The Reinforcement Learning Process

The RL process typically involves the following steps:

1. **Initialization:** The agent starts with an initial policy and value function.

2. **Interaction:** The agent interacts with the environment, observes the state, takes an action, and receives a reward.

3. **Learning:** The agent updates its policy and value function based on the received reward and observed state.

4. **Iteration:** The process repeats, with the agent continuously improving its policy to maximize cumulative rewards.

Types of Reinforcement Learning

There are several types of reinforcement learning algorithms, including:

1. **Model-Free RL:** The agent learns directly from interactions with the environment without an explicit model of the environment. Examples include Q-learning and SARSA.

2. **Model-Based RL:** The agent builds a model of the environment to predict future states and rewards, improving decision-making. Examples include Dyna-Q

and Monte Carlo Tree Search.

3. **Policy Gradient Methods:** The agent directly learns the policy by optimizing the expected cumulative reward using gradient ascent techniques. Examples include REINFORCE and Actor-Critic methods.

Applications of Reinforcement Learning

RL has a wide range of applications across various domains:

1. **Gaming:** Training agents to play and excel in complex games such as chess, Go, and video games.
2. **Robotics:** Enabling robots to learn tasks such as grasping objects, navigating environments, and performing complex manipulations.
3. **Finance:** Optimizing trading strategies, portfolio management, and automated market making.
4. **Healthcare:** Personalizing treatment plans, optimizing resource allocation, and assisting in medical diagnosis.
5. **Transportation:** Developing autonomous vehicles, optimizing traffic flow, and improving logistics and supply chain management.

Challenges in Reinforcement Learning

Despite its potential, RL faces several challenges:

1. **Exploration vs. Exploitation:** Balancing the need to explore new actions to discover better rewards with the need to exploit known actions to maximize rewards.
2. **Sample Efficiency:** RL algorithms often require a large number of interactions with the environment to learn effectively, which can be impractical in real-world scenarios.
3. **Credit Assignment:** Determining which actions are

responsible for observed rewards, especially in environments with delayed feedback.

4. **Stability and Convergence:** Ensuring that RL algorithms converge to optimal policies and remain stable during training.

Future Directions in Reinforcement Learning

The future of RL holds exciting possibilities:

1. **Hierarchical RL:** Developing algorithms that learn hierarchical policies, breaking down complex tasks into simpler sub-tasks.

2. **Multi-Agent RL:** Training multiple agents to cooperate or compete in shared environments, enabling applications such as autonomous vehicle coordination and multi-robot systems.

3. **Transfer Learning:** Leveraging knowledge from previously learned tasks to improve learning efficiency in new tasks.

4. **Safe and Robust RL:** Ensuring that RL agents operate safely and robustly in real-world environments, addressing issues such as risk aversion and robustness to uncertainty.

Conclusion

Reinforcement learning is a powerful and versatile approach to training agents for decision-making tasks. By understanding the principles, key components, and applications of RL, we can harness its potential to solve complex problems across various domains. As the field continues to advance, addressing the challenges and exploring new directions will be crucial for further progress and impactful applications.

CHAPTER 7:
COMPUTER VISION

Computer Vision is a subfield of AI that focuses on enabling machines to interpret and understand visual information from the world. This chapter explores the fundamental concepts, techniques, and applications of computer vision.

What is Computer Vision?

Computer vision involves the development of algorithms and models that allow computers to process, analyze, and understand images and videos. It encompasses a wide range of tasks, including:

1. **Image Classification:** Assigning labels to images based on their content.
2. **Object Detection:** Identifying and locating objects within images.
3. **Image Segmentation:** Dividing an image into segments to simplify analysis.
4. **Face Recognition:** Identifying and verifying individuals based on facial features.
5. **Action Recognition:** Recognizing actions and activities in video sequences.

Key Techniques in Computer Vision

Several techniques are commonly used in computer vision, including:

1. **Convolutional Neural Networks (CNNs):** Specialized neural networks that are highly effective for image-related tasks due to their ability to capture spatial hierarchies.

2. **Feature Extraction:** Identifying important features in images, such as edges, textures, and shapes, to facilitate analysis.

3. **Image Preprocessing:** Techniques such as normalization, resizing, and augmentation to prepare images for analysis.

4. **Transfer Learning:** Leveraging pre-trained models on large datasets to improve performance on specific tasks with limited data.

Computer Vision Algorithms and Models

Computer vision relies on various algorithms and models to perform its tasks:

1. **Haar Cascades:** A machine learning-based approach for object detection, particularly for detecting faces in images.

2. **YOLO (You Only Look Once):** A real-time object detection system that divides images into grids and predicts bounding boxes and class probabilities for each grid cell.

3. **Mask R-CNN:** An extension of Faster R-CNN that adds a branch for predicting segmentation masks in addition to bounding boxes.

4. **OpenPose:** A system for real-time multi-person keypoint detection, useful for tasks such as human pose estimation.

Applications of Computer Vision

Computer vision has numerous applications across different industries:

1. **Healthcare:** Medical image analysis for disease diagnosis, treatment planning, and surgery assistance.
2. **Retail:** Automated checkout systems, inventory management, and customer behavior analysis.
3. **Autonomous Vehicles:** Perception systems for detecting and recognizing objects, lane markings, and pedestrians.
4. **Security:** Surveillance systems, facial recognition for authentication, and anomaly detection.
5. **Entertainment:** Augmented reality (AR), virtual reality (VR), and visual effects in movies and games.

Challenges in Computer Vision

Computer vision faces several challenges that researchers and practitioners must address:

1. **Data Diversity:** Variations in lighting, perspective, and occlusion can affect the accuracy of computer vision models.
2. **Real-Time Processing:** Ensuring that computer vision systems can process and analyze visual data in real-time for applications such as autonomous driving.
3. **Generalization:** Developing models that generalize well to new, unseen data, reducing the need for extensive retraining.
4. **Ethical Considerations:** Ensuring the ethical use of computer vision technologies, addressing issues such as privacy, bias, and consent.

Future Directions in Computer Vision

The future of computer vision holds promising developments:

1. **3D Vision:** Advancing techniques for 3D object

detection, reconstruction, and understanding, enabling applications such as AR and robotics.

2. **Few-Shot Learning:** Developing models that can learn from a small number of examples, reducing the reliance on large labeled datasets.

3. **Explainable Vision:** Creating models that provide interpretable and understandable explanations for their decisions, enhancing trust and transparency.

4. **Human-AI Collaboration:** Improving the ability of computer vision systems to work collaboratively with humans, augmenting human capabilities and enhancing decision-making processes.

Conclusion

Computer vision is a critical area of AI that enables machines to interpret and understand visual information from the world. By exploring the fundamental concepts, techniques, and applications of computer vision, we gain insights into how this technology is transforming various industries and improving our daily lives. As the field continues to advance, addressing the challenges and exploring new directions will be essential for further progress and impactful applications.

CHAPTER 8: ETHICAL AND SOCIETAL IMPLICATIONS OF AI

As AI technologies become increasingly integrated into our daily lives, it is crucial to consider the ethical and societal implications of their use. This chapter explores the key ethical issues, potential societal impacts, and guidelines for responsible AI development and deployment.

Key Ethical Issues in AI

Several ethical issues arise from the use of AI technologies:

1. **Bias and Fairness:** AI systems can perpetuate or even amplify existing biases present in the training data, leading to unfair treatment of certain groups.

2. **Privacy:** The collection and use of personal data by AI systems raise significant privacy concerns, particularly in areas such as surveillance and targeted advertising.

3. **Transparency and Accountability:** AI systems often operate as "black boxes," making it difficult to understand how decisions are made and who is responsible for the outcomes.

4. **Autonomy and Control:** The increasing autonomy of AI systems raises questions about human control and oversight, particularly in high-stakes areas such as healthcare and autonomous vehicles.

CHAPTER 9: AI IN HEALTHCARE

Artificial Intelligence (AI) has the potential to revolutionize healthcare by enhancing diagnosis, treatment, and patient care. This chapter delves into the various applications of AI in healthcare, the benefits it offers, and the challenges it faces.

AI Applications in Healthcare

AI is being utilized in numerous ways to improve healthcare outcomes:

1. **Medical Imaging:** AI algorithms can analyze medical images, such as X-rays, MRIs, and CT scans, to detect abnormalities and assist in diagnosis. Deep learning models, particularly convolutional neural networks (CNNs), have shown remarkable accuracy in identifying conditions such as tumors, fractures, and infections.

2. **Predictive Analytics:** AI can analyze vast amounts of patient data to predict disease outbreaks, patient readmissions, and the likelihood of developing certain conditions. This predictive capability allows for proactive interventions and personalized treatment plans.

3. **Drug Discovery:** AI accelerates the drug discovery process by analyzing biological data to identify potential drug candidates. Machine learning models can predict how new drugs will interact with targets and simulate clinical trials to identify promising

compounds faster than traditional methods.

4. **Virtual Health Assistants:** AI-powered virtual assistants can provide patients with instant medical advice, schedule appointments, and offer reminders for medication. These assistants help reduce the burden on healthcare providers and improve patient engagement.

5. **Electronic Health Records (EHRs):** AI can streamline the management of EHRs by automating data entry, extracting relevant information, and providing insights for clinical decision-making. Natural language processing (NLP) techniques are particularly useful in analyzing unstructured data in EHRs.

Benefits of AI in Healthcare

AI offers several benefits that can transform healthcare delivery:

1. **Improved Diagnosis and Treatment:** AI's ability to analyze large datasets and recognize patterns can lead to more accurate and early diagnoses, enabling timely and effective treatment.

2. **Personalized Medicine:** AI can tailor treatment plans to individual patients based on their genetic makeup, lifestyle, and medical history, leading to more effective and personalized care.

3. **Operational Efficiency:** AI can automate routine tasks, reduce administrative burdens, and optimize resource allocation, leading to cost savings and improved operational efficiency.

4. **Enhanced Patient Experience:** AI-powered tools can improve patient engagement and satisfaction by providing personalized care, reducing wait times, and offering convenient access to medical information.

Challenges of AI in Healthcare

Despite its potential, AI in healthcare faces several challenges:

1. **Data Privacy and Security:** The use of AI requires access to vast amounts of patient data, raising concerns about data privacy and security. Ensuring that patient information is protected and used ethically is paramount.

2. **Regulatory and Ethical Issues:** The deployment of AI in healthcare must comply with regulatory standards and ethical guidelines. This includes ensuring transparency, accountability, and fairness in AI algorithms.

3. **Integration with Existing Systems:** Integrating AI into existing healthcare systems can be challenging due to compatibility issues, the need for infrastructure upgrades, and resistance to change from healthcare professionals.

4. **Bias and Fairness:** AI algorithms can inherit biases present in training data, leading to disparities in healthcare outcomes. Addressing these biases and ensuring fair treatment for all patients is essential.

5. **Trust and Adoption:** Gaining the trust of healthcare providers and patients is crucial for the widespread adoption of AI. This requires demonstrating the reliability, accuracy, and benefits of AI applications.

Future Directions in AI for Healthcare

The future of AI in healthcare is promising, with several exciting developments on the horizon:

1. **AI-Driven Genomics:** AI will play a crucial role in analyzing genomic data, leading to advancements in precision medicine and the development of targeted therapies for genetic disorders.

2. **AI in Surgery:** AI-powered robotic systems will enhance surgical precision, reduce recovery times, and improve patient outcomes. These systems can assist surgeons in complex procedures and provide real-time insights

during operations.

3. **Remote Monitoring and Telemedicine:** AI will enable remote patient monitoring and telemedicine, allowing for continuous health tracking and virtual consultations. This will be particularly beneficial for patients in remote or underserved areas.

4. **AI in Mental Health:** AI can analyze patterns in speech, text, and behavior to detect early signs of mental health conditions and provide timely interventions. Virtual therapists and chatbots can offer support and resources to individuals seeking help.

5. **Collaboration Between Humans and AI:** The future of healthcare will see increased collaboration between healthcare professionals and AI systems. AI will augment human capabilities, providing support and insights to improve clinical decision-making.

Conclusion

AI has the potential to transform healthcare by improving diagnosis, treatment, and patient care. By exploring the various applications, benefits, and challenges of AI in healthcare, we gain insights into how this technology can enhance healthcare delivery and outcomes. As the field continues to advance, addressing the challenges and exploring new directions will be essential for realizing the full potential of AI in healthcare.

CHAPTER 10: AI
IN FINANCE

Artificial Intelligence (AI) is reshaping the financial industry by enhancing decision-making, improving customer service, and optimizing operations. This chapter explores the key applications of AI in finance, the benefits it offers, and the challenges it faces.

AI Applications in Finance

AI is being utilized in numerous ways to improve financial services:

1. **Algorithmic Trading:** AI algorithms can analyze market data and execute trades at high speeds, taking advantage of market fluctuations to generate profits. Machine learning models can identify patterns and make predictions to inform trading strategies.

2. **Fraud Detection:** AI can detect fraudulent activities by analyzing transaction patterns and identifying anomalies. Machine learning models can continuously learn from new data to improve the accuracy of fraud detection.

3. **Credit Scoring:** AI can assess creditworthiness by analyzing a wide range of data, including financial history, spending behavior, and social media activity. This enables more accurate and fair credit scoring, particularly for individuals with limited credit history.

4. **Risk Management:** AI can identify and assess risks by analyzing financial data, market trends, and economic

indicators. This helps financial institutions make informed decisions and mitigate potential risks.

5. **Customer Service:** AI-powered chatbots and virtual assistants can provide personalized financial advice, answer customer queries, and assist with transactions. This enhances customer experience and reduces the workload on customer service teams.

6. **Financial Forecasting:** AI can analyze historical data and market trends to make accurate financial forecasts. This helps businesses plan for the future and make informed investment decisions.

Benefits of AI in Finance

AI offers several benefits that can transform the financial industry:

1. **Enhanced Decision-Making:** AI's ability to analyze large datasets and identify patterns enables more accurate and data-driven decision-making.

2. **Improved Efficiency:** AI can automate routine tasks, reduce operational costs, and optimize processes, leading to increased efficiency and productivity.

3. **Personalized Services:** AI can provide personalized financial advice and services based on individual customer needs and preferences, enhancing customer satisfaction.

4. **Fraud Prevention:** AI's ability to detect and prevent fraudulent activities helps protect financial institutions and their customers from financial losses.

5. **Risk Mitigation:** AI can identify and assess risks more accurately, enabling financial institutions to take proactive measures to mitigate potential risks.

Challenges of AI in Finance

Despite its potential, AI in finance faces several challenges:

1. **Data Privacy and Security:** The use of AI requires access to vast amounts of financial data, raising concerns about data privacy and security. Ensuring that customer information is protected and used ethically is paramount.

2. **Regulatory Compliance:** The deployment of AI in finance must comply with regulatory standards and guidelines. This includes ensuring transparency, accountability, and fairness in AI algorithms.

3. **Bias and Fairness:** AI algorithms can inherit biases present in training data, leading to disparities in financial services. Addressing these biases and ensuring fair treatment for all customers is essential.

4. **Integration with Legacy Systems:** Integrating AI into existing financial systems can be challenging due to compatibility issues, the need for infrastructure upgrades, and resistance to change from financial professionals.

5. **Trust and Adoption:** Gaining the trust of financial institutions and customers is crucial for the widespread adoption of AI. This requires demonstrating the reliability, accuracy, and benefits of AI applications.

Future Directions in AI for Finance

The future of AI in finance is promising, with several exciting developments on the horizon:

1. **AI-Driven Wealth Management:** AI will play a crucial role in wealth management by providing personalized investment advice and portfolio management. AI-driven robo-advisors will help individuals make informed investment decisions.

2. **Blockchain and AI Integration:** The integration of AI with blockchain technology will enhance transparency, security, and efficiency in financial transactions.

This will be particularly beneficial for cross-border payments and supply chain finance.

3. **AI in Regulatory Technology (RegTech):** AI will help financial institutions comply with regulatory requirements by automating compliance processes and detecting potential violations. This will reduce the burden of regulatory compliance and enhance transparency.

4. **AI in Insurance:** AI will transform the insurance industry by enabling more accurate risk assessment, personalized insurance products, and faster claims processing. AI-driven underwriting will improve the efficiency and accuracy of insurance policies.

5. **Ethical AI in Finance:** The future of AI in finance will focus on developing ethical AI frameworks to ensure fairness, transparency, and accountability. This will address issues such as bias, discrimination, and privacy concerns.

Conclusion

AI has the potential to transform the financial industry by enhancing decision-making, improving customer service, and optimizing operations. By exploring the various applications, benefits, and challenges of AI in finance, we gain insights into how this technology can enhance financial services and outcomes. As the field continues to advance, addressing the challenges and exploring new directions will be essential for realizing the full potential of AI in finance.

CHAPTER 11: AI
IN EDUCATION

Artificial Intelligence (AI) is poised to revolutionize education by personalizing learning experiences, improving teaching methods, and enhancing administrative processes. This chapter delves into the various applications of AI in education, the benefits it offers, and the challenges it faces.

AI Applications in Education

AI is being utilized in numerous ways to improve educational outcomes:

1. **Personalized Learning:** AI can create personalized learning pathways for students based on their individual needs, strengths, and weaknesses. Adaptive learning platforms use AI to adjust the content and pace of learning, ensuring that each student receives a tailored educational experience.

2. **Intelligent Tutoring Systems:** AI-powered tutoring systems can provide one-on-one support to students, offering explanations, feedback, and guidance. These systems can adapt to the student's learning style and provide targeted assistance to help them master difficult concepts.

3. **Automated Grading:** AI can automate the grading of assignments, quizzes, and exams, reducing the workload on teachers and providing timely feedback to students. Machine learning models can evaluate open-

ended responses, essays, and even code submissions.

4. **Virtual Classrooms:** AI can enhance virtual classrooms by providing interactive and immersive learning experiences. Virtual assistants can facilitate discussions, answer questions, and provide real-time support to students.

5. **Administrative Automation:** AI can streamline administrative tasks such as enrollment, scheduling, and resource allocation. This improves operational efficiency and allows educators to focus more on teaching and student engagement.

6. **Early Intervention:** AI can analyze student data to identify those at risk of falling behind or dropping out. Early intervention programs can then provide targeted support and resources to help these students succeed.

Benefits of AI in Education

AI offers several benefits that can transform education:

1. **Personalized Learning Experiences:** AI can tailor educational content to individual students, ensuring that each learner receives the support and challenge they need to thrive.

2. **Improved Student Engagement:** AI-powered tools can make learning more interactive and engaging, keeping students motivated and interested in their studies.

3. **Enhanced Teaching Methods:** AI can provide teachers with insights into student performance and learning patterns, enabling them to adjust their teaching methods to better meet the needs of their students.

4. **Operational Efficiency:** AI can automate routine administrative tasks, freeing up time and resources for more impactful activities such as curriculum development and student support.

5. **Data-Driven Decision Making:** AI can analyze vast

amounts of educational data to inform decision-making at all levels, from individual classrooms to entire school districts.

Challenges of AI in Education

Despite its potential, AI in education faces several challenges:

1. **Data Privacy and Security:** The use of AI requires access to sensitive student data, raising concerns about data privacy and security. Ensuring that student information is protected and used ethically is paramount.

2. **Equity and Access:** There is a risk that AI could exacerbate existing educational inequalities if access to AI-powered tools and resources is not evenly distributed. Ensuring equitable access to AI technologies is essential.

3. **Bias and Fairness:** AI algorithms can inherit biases present in training data, leading to disparities in educational outcomes. Addressing these biases and ensuring fair treatment for all students is crucial.

4. **Teacher Training and Support:** Educators need training and support to effectively integrate AI into their teaching practices. Professional development programs should focus on building AI literacy and skills.

5. **Trust and Adoption:** Gaining the trust of educators, students, and parents is crucial for the widespread adoption of AI in education. This requires demonstrating the reliability, accuracy, and benefits of AI applications.

Future Directions in AI for Education

The future of AI in education is promising, with several exciting developments on the horizon:

1. **AI-Driven Assessment:** AI will play a crucial role in

developing more sophisticated and accurate assessment methods that go beyond traditional testing. These assessments will provide a comprehensive view of student learning and progress.

2. **Lifelong Learning:** AI will support lifelong learning by providing personalized learning experiences and resources for individuals of all ages. This will enable continuous skill development and career advancement.

3. **AI in Curriculum Development:** AI will assist in curriculum development by analyzing educational trends, identifying skill gaps, and suggesting relevant content. This will ensure that curricula are up-to-date and aligned with the needs of the workforce.

4. **AI in Special Education:** AI will enhance special education by providing tailored support and resources for students with disabilities. This includes adaptive learning tools, communication aids, and assistive technologies.

5. **Global Collaboration:** AI will facilitate global collaboration among educators, researchers, and policymakers, enabling the sharing of best practices, resources, and innovations in education.

Conclusion

AI has the potential to transform education by personalizing learning experiences, improving teaching methods, and enhancing administrative processes. By exploring the various applications, benefits, and challenges of AI in education, we gain insights into how this technology can enhance educational outcomes. As the field continues to advance, addressing the challenges and exploring new directions will be essential for realizing the full potential of AI in education.

CHAPTER 12: AI IN TRANSPORTATION

Artificial Intelligence (AI) is set to revolutionize the transportation industry by improving safety, efficiency, and sustainability. This chapter explores the key applications of AI in transportation, the benefits it offers, and the challenges it faces.

AI Applications in Transportation

AI is being utilized in numerous ways to improve transportation systems:

1. **Autonomous Vehicles:** AI enables the development of self-driving cars, trucks, and buses. These vehicles use sensors, cameras, and AI algorithms to navigate and make real-time decisions, reducing the need for human drivers.

2. **Traffic Management:** AI can analyze traffic patterns and optimize traffic flow to reduce congestion and improve travel times. This includes smart traffic lights, predictive analytics, and real-time traffic monitoring.

3. **Fleet Management:** AI can optimize fleet operations by analyzing data on vehicle performance, routes, and maintenance needs. This helps reduce costs, improve efficiency, and extend the lifespan of vehicles.

4. **Predictive Maintenance:** AI can predict when vehicles and infrastructure components are likely to fail, allowing for proactive maintenance. This reduces downtime, prevents accidents, and lowers maintenance

costs.

5. **Public Transportation:** AI can enhance public transportation systems by optimizing routes, schedules, and capacity. This improves service reliability and passenger satisfaction.

6. **Logistics and Supply Chain:** AI can streamline logistics and supply chain operations by optimizing routes, managing inventory, and predicting demand. This reduces costs and improves efficiency.

Benefits of AI in Transportation

AI offers several benefits that can transform the transportation industry:

1. **Improved Safety:** AI can enhance safety by reducing human errors, predicting and preventing accidents, and optimizing maintenance schedules.

2. **Increased Efficiency:** AI can optimize routes, reduce congestion, and streamline operations, leading to increased efficiency and reduced costs.

3. **Enhanced User Experience:** AI can provide personalized travel recommendations, real-time information, and improved service reliability, enhancing the overall user experience.

4. **Environmental Sustainability:** AI can promote sustainable transportation by optimizing fuel consumption, reducing emissions, and supporting the adoption of electric and autonomous vehicles.

5. **Operational Flexibility:** AI can enable more flexible and adaptive transportation systems that can respond to changing conditions and demands.

Challenges of AI in Transportation

Despite its potential, AI in transportation faces several challenges:

1. **Safety and Reliability:** Ensuring the safety and reliability of AI systems, particularly in autonomous vehicles, is critical. This includes addressing technical challenges and ensuring compliance with safety regulations.

2. **Data Privacy and Security:** The use of AI requires access to vast amounts of data, raising concerns about data privacy and security. Ensuring that data is protected and used ethically is paramount.

3. **Regulatory and Legal Issues:** The deployment of AI in transportation must comply with regulatory standards and legal frameworks. This includes addressing liability issues and ensuring that AI systems are accountable.

4. **Infrastructure Upgrades:** Integrating AI into transportation systems may require significant infrastructure upgrades, including new sensors, communication networks, and data management systems.

5. **Public Acceptance:** Gaining public acceptance and trust in AI-powered transportation systems is crucial for widespread adoption. This requires demonstrating the safety, reliability, and benefits of these systems.

Future Directions in AI for Transportation

The future of AI in transportation is promising, with several exciting developments on the horizon:

1. **Fully Autonomous Vehicles:** The development of fully autonomous vehicles that can operate safely and efficiently without human intervention is a major focus of AI research. This includes advancements in sensor technology, machine learning, and regulatory frameworks.

2. **Smart Cities:** AI will play a crucial role in developing

smart cities with integrated transportation systems that optimize traffic flow, reduce congestion, and enhance mobility. This includes the use of AI for urban planning, public transportation, and infrastructure management.

3. **Connected Vehicles:** The integration of AI with Internet of Things (IoT) technology will enable connected vehicles that can communicate with each other and with infrastructure components. This will improve safety, efficiency, and real-time decision-making.

4. **Electric and Sustainable Transportation:** AI will support the transition to electric and sustainable transportation by optimizing battery management, charging infrastructure, and energy consumption. This will reduce environmental impact and promote sustainability.

5. **AI-Driven Logistics:** AI will transform logistics and supply chain management by enabling real-time tracking, predictive analytics, and automated decision-making. This will improve efficiency, reduce costs, and enhance customer satisfaction.

Conclusion

AI has the potential to revolutionize the transportation industry by improving safety, efficiency, and sustainability. By exploring the various applications, benefits, and challenges of AI in transportation, we gain insights into how this technology can enhance transportation systems and outcomes. As the field continues to advance, addressing the challenges and exploring new directions will be essential for realizing the full potential of AI in transportation.

www.ingramcontent.com/pod-product-compliance
Lightning Source LLC
LaVergne TN
LVHW051618050326
832903LV00033B/4553